Margaret Davidson

True Animal Stories

Illustrated by Pauline Hazelwood

Hippo Books
Scholastic Publications Limited
London

Scholastic Publications Ltd,
10 Earlham Street, London WC2H 9RX, UK

Scholastic Inc,
730 Broadway, New York, NY 10003, USA

Scholastic Tab Publications Ltd,
123 Newkirk Road, Richmond Hill,
Ontario L4C 3G5, Canada

Ashton Scholastic Pty Ltd,
P O Box 579, Gosford, New South Wales,
Australia

Ashton Scholastic Ltd,
165 Marua Road, Panmure, Auckland 6,
New Zealand

This edition first published by Scholastic Publications Ltd, 1990
This edition is a selection of stories from three books first published by
Scholastic Inc.
Five True Dog Stories, 1977
Five True Horse Stories, 1979
Nine True Dolphin Stories, 1974

ISBN 0 590 76289 3

Made and printed by Cox and Wyman Ltd,
Reading, Berks

Typeset in Baskerville by COLLAGE (Design in Print)
Longfield Hill, Kent

10 9 8 7 6 5 4 3 2 1

CONTENTS

1

Dox – the greatest dog detective in the world

The policeman just happened to be passing a pet shop one day. He looked in and saw a roly-poly Alsatian pup in the window. And the pup looked back at him. The man wasn't even thinking of buying a dog. But a few minutes later he came out of the shop with the dog in his arms. "It was love at first sight," Giovanni Maimone told his friends. And he named his new pet Dox.

Maimone worked as a policeman in the city of Turin, Italy. He decided to train Dox to help him in his work. Dox was a very clever dog. And, like most dogs, he had a good sense of smell. Maimone wanted to train Dox to find hidden things — jewels or money or people.

Maimone worked with Dox as much as he could. First he took a handkerchief and a cigarette case. They both belonged to someone Dox didn't know. And they carried

the person's own special smell. Maimone hid the cigarette case behind the cushion of a big overstuffed chair. He let Dox sniff the handkerchief. "Find it, boy!" he said.

Of course Dox didn't understand — not at first. So Maimone led the dog to the overstuffed chair. He lifted the cushion — and there was the cigarette case. Dox sniffed at it. "Good boy!" Maimone said — as if Dox had found it by himself.

Very soon Dox understood exactly what was going on. Every time his master asked him to sniff something and then said, "Find it!" Dox knew he must find something that smelled the same.

Of course it was still just a game they were playing. Then one day a jewellery shop was robbed. The thief escaped with many fine jewels. He'd left nothing behind — except a dirty old glove. Maimone decided to take Dox along. It was time to test the dog on a real case.

When they got to the jewellery shop, several other policemen were already there. One looked up and said with a grin, "Oh, I see you've brought Dox. Do you think he can lend us a paw?"

Everyone laughed. Everyone except Maimone. Quietly he asked for the glove. He let Dox sniff it. Then he said, "Find him, Dox!"

First Dox sniffed across the floor of the jewellery shop. Out of the door he ran, followed by Maimone and several other policemen. Dox moved slowly but steadily for several blocks. Then he came to a main road. He started to go down it one way. He stopped. The busy road was filled with so many smells — petrol fumes and grass and rubber tyres and trees. How could he possibly find the special glove smell?

But he did. Dox sniffed by the side of the road for a minute or two. Then he set off in the other direction. He never lost the trail again. At last he turned off the main road into a narrow side street. Dox led the men to one of the houses on the street and sat down on the porch.

Maimone knocked on the door. His knock was answered by a woman with a baby in her arms. "What do you want?" she snapped.

The policemen explained. "There's no one else here," she answered. "Except for *her* . . . " She jiggled the baby in her arms. "My husband's in jail."

But Maimone was still suspicious. After all, Dox had led them right to this house. He and the other policemen kept checking. They soon found out that the woman was lying. Her husband had been in jail. But he was now out. A few days later the police caught him in a nearby town. He soon admitted that he had robbed the jewellery shop. Then he had gone home for a few minutes to say goodbye to his wife and child.

Dox had solved his first case!

So the career of Dox, the dog detective, began. Before long the police in other towns heard about Dox. Often they asked for his help. He worked with the police all over Italy.

Other people knew the big dog too. Some of Dox's best friends were restaurant owners.

On his birthday he could eat all he wanted in any one of their restaurants — free of charge.

Maimone would lead him from one place to another. At each door Dox would stop and sniff. He'd move on until he found one that seemed to have nicer smells than all the rest. Then he would go in for his favourite birthday dinner of spaghetti and pork.

On Dox's thirteenth birthday Maimone led him from restaurant to restaurant as usual. Dox seemed to be having an especially hard time deciding this year. "Choose, will

you?" Maimone finally begged. "*I'm* getting hungry."

Just then he came to a small restaurant. Dox took a deep sniff. He became very still. Only his nose continued to twitch. He quickly pushed open the door and went inside.

But Dox wasn't interested in food. Not now. He headed straight for a man who was sitting at a small corner table. The man kept on shovelling food into his mouth. He tried very hard to pretend he hadn't seen Dox. It was no use. Maimone recognized the man

right away. He was a criminal who had escaped from the police a long time ago. He was caught now — because Dox had remembered his human smell for more than *six* years.

Year after year Dox did his job. In fifteen years he helped catch more than 400 criminals!

"He has probably cracked more cases than any detective on the force," one police officer said. "We consider him one of our best men."

2

Grip – the dog who was a thief

Grip was a friendly dog. And a friendly dog was just what Tom Gerrard wanted — for Tom Gerrard was a thief. He lived in the city of London more than three hundred years ago. Sometimes Tom Gerrard robbed big houses and shops. But most of all he liked to steal from people. That's what he trained Grip to do — to pick people's pockets.

The man and the dog would hide in an alley near a busy London street, and wait. They would wait until a man or woman came by — a well-dressed person who might be carrying a lot of money.

Tom would point at the person and softly snap his fingers. Grip would then trot out of the alley and begin a happy dog's dance in front of the victim.

He frisked, he wriggled, he wagged his tail. Sometimes the people just pushed past. But most people stopped to pet the friendly dog.

This was just what Grip had been waiting for. He would continue to prance and wriggle. But he was also using his nose to sniff out the smell of leather — the smell of a purse full of money.

It never took Grip long to find what he was looking for. Then his big mouth would open and close over the pocket with the purse in it. And with one powerful tug he'd tear the pocket and purse away from the person's clothes!

Then Grip would dash away — leaving the poor victim standing open-mouthed. "Hey, you! Stop!" they usually shouted. And the chase would begin.

Some of the people could run very fast. But Grip was never caught. He knew just where to go. He knew all the twisting streets and narrow alleys of London. He'd race up one and down another. Sometimes he would hide in a dark doorway until the pursuer ran by. Then Grip would come out — and run the other way!

Grip always kept running until he was sure he was safe. Finally, with the purse held firmly in his teeth, he would go back to the first alley where his master was waiting for him.

"Good dog, Grip!" Tom Gerrard always said as the dog dropped the purse into his hand. These few words of praise were all the reward Grip worked for.

What a team they made — the thief and the dog! Probably Tom Gerrard could have gone on stealing for many more years — if he'd been content just to pick pockets.

But Tom was a greedy man. One raw and windy night he stopped a stagecoach on a road outside town. The door of the coach burst open. Three men with guns jumped out. Tom didn't stand a chance. He was captured and thrown into jail.

Poor Grip. For the next few weeks he wandered about the streets of London. The only food he ate was scraps of rubbish. And he slept in doorways or dirty alleys.

Then one day Grip saw a man walking down the street. He trotted up to him — and the man patted his head. That was all the lonely dog needed. He followed the man home.

But who was this man Grip had chosen to be his new master? Was he another thief, like Tom Gerrard? Not at all.

The man he picked to be his new master turned out to be the minister of a church instead!

3

Wolf – the dog who saved other dogs

Wolf was not a friendly dog. He loved his master and mistress very much, but he didn't like other people. Wolf didn't seem to like other dogs either. He hardly ever played with the other collies that lived with him at Sunnybank Farm.

Wolf didn't like other dogs much, but he seemed to feel he had to take care of them. A big sign at the beginning of the farm's long, curving drive read: "GO SLOW! DOGS RUNNING FREE!" Still, cars and lorries would often come roaring up the drive.

Once a litter of pups chose the middle of the drive as their playground. So for hours at a time poor Wolf lay on the grass nearby. He

watched the puppies race and tumble up and down the drive. Every time he heard a car turn in from the road he got up and circled round and round the pups until they were in a tight bunch. Then he herded them off the drive.

But Wolf couldn't watch the puppies all the time. One day they were playing in the drive as usual. A delivery lorry turned into the farm. It swept around the first curve and came racing towards the pups.

Just then Wolf came out of a clump of trees across the lawn. He saw the danger the puppies were in. But the lorry was coming so fast! And he was too far away to get them out of the way in time!

Wolf began to bark. He dashed a little way towards the dogs. Still barking, he swung around and raced towards the trees again.

"*Come on, everyone*! *Chase me*!" his loud bark seemed to be saying. And one after another the puppies did run after Wolf — off the drive and away from the lorry.

So the years passed peacefully at Sunnybank Farm. Wolf continued to watch over dogs who couldn't take care of themselves. The rest of the time he went his own way.

Wolf especially liked to take long walks. One warm spring afternoon he took a walk that led him to a railway line.

Wolf knew about roads and cars. He also knew about railway lines and trains. He would look in both directions and listen hard. Then he quickly crossed to the other side.

He did this now. He looked left and then right. He cocked his head. There was no train to be seen. But Wolf sat down to wait anyway. He must have heard the sound of a whistle in the distance.

A little brown dog walked past Wolf. The dog didn't look. He didn't listen either. He just walked on to the tracks and sat down to scratch a few fleas.

Wolf sprang up. He barked in warning. The dog just went on scratching. Then the sound of the train's whistle came again — much louder this time. And the train swept into sight!

Finally the little brown dog looked up. But *still* he didn't move. Now Wolf jumped and threw himself against the little dog. The dog flew through the air and landed in a nearby ditch.

Wolf tried to leap into the ditch too. He almost made it. But not quite. A piece of metal on the engine hit the side of his head. Wolf lay by the tracks. The dog who didn't like other dogs very much would never move again. He had given his life to save a stranger.

4

Barry – the dog who saved people

Today fine roads lead over the high mountains of Switzerland. Snow ploughs keep the roads open even in the worst weather. But it wasn't always this way.

Before the roads were built it was often very hard to cross over the mountains in winter. The only way was through some of the passes — pathways between the high peaks. One of these passes was the Great St Bernard Pass. At the highest point of the pass stood a big stone building. This was the monastery of Great St Bernard. Monks had lived here for hundreds of years. They helped people travel safely in the mountains.

Sometimes the monks led travellers along the narrow path through the pass. And sometimes, when wild storms raged, they searched for those who might be lost.

This could be very dangerous work. But the monks had help. A group of big, shaggy dogs called St Bernards also lived at the monastery. This is the story of one of those dogs. Barry was his name.

Barry was born in the spring of 1800. At first he romped and rolled with his brothers and sisters. He tagged after the bigger dogs. And he ate and slept whenever he felt like it.

But soon the short mountain summer was over. The first snow fell. It was time for Barry and the other young St Bernards to go to school. They had some very important lessons to learn.

First Barry had to learn to obey. He learned to come when the monks called him, to sit and lie down when the monks told him to. He learned how to walk in the deep snow. He learned how to turn his big paws outward — and spread the pads of his paws to keep from sinking in the snow. At first he still sank in up to his belly. But after a while he could walk on the snowy crust without breaking through.

Now it was time for harder lessons. Barry learned to lead people through the pass even when the narrow path was buried under many metres of snow. And he learned one of the hardest lessons of all — to find people who might be lost in a storm.

If the person could walk, Barry led him back to the monastery. But sometimes a person would be hurt — or weakened by the cold. Then Barry raced back to the monastery to lead the monks back to the spot.

He also learned to search for people who were lost *under* the snow. Sometimes an avalanche — a great slide of snow — would break free from one of the high peaks. It would come crashing down the mountain and bury anyone who was in its path.

The dogs were especially important at times like this. A dog could smell people even when they were buried under many metres of snow. Then he would bark loudly, and the monks would come running.

All winter Barry and the other dogs learned their lessons. And before long the monks began to watch Barry very carefully. There was something special about the dog. He learned much faster than the others. But that was not enough. Would Barry be brave? Could the monks trust him as a rescue dog?

At last the lessons were over, and Barry went to work. One afternoon he was trotting ahead of a long line of workmen, leading them through the pass. There was a loud booming noise. It was the beginning of an avalanche!

Barry had never heard this sound before. But somehow he knew that something terrible was about to happen. He raced ahead, barking. Then he circled back around the men. He was trying to get them to move faster. And the men tried. But the last three didn't make it. Moments later the avalanche rolled down over the trail — and the three men were buried under it.

Barry knew that they were probably still alive. It was possible to breathe under snow, but not for long.

Barry looked at the snowy spot for a moment. Then he bounded away. A few minutes later he dashed into the courtyard of the monastery. The monks came running when they heard his frantic barks. "*It's trouble I can't handle alone!*" those barks meant. "*Follow me!*" Then he started out into the snow again.

The monks followed Barry back to where the avalanche had slid across the path. And the men who had got through safely told them what had happened.

"Find them, Barry," a monk ordered. Barry began to sniff across the snow. Suddenly he barked. One of the monks ran over. Carefully he poked a long pole down into the snow. He moved a few metres and poked again. Still nothing. So he tried a third time — and gave a shout. "Here!"

Other monks began to dig. A few minutes later the man was free. He was shivering and blue with cold, but he was alive! Soon the other two men were saved too.

That night everyone — the monks and the rescued men — made a big fuss over Barry. They praised him. They petted him. They gave him a large bowl of juicy meat scraps. And the monks nodded to one another. They had been right. This was going to be a *very* special dog.

One day Barry was out on patrol. He saw a small mound of snow. Something was sticking out of that mound — something that looked like the end of a red scarf. Barry raced over. He saw now that the mound was a little girl! She lay curled up in the snow. Barry poked her. Was she still alive? She was. But the cold had made her very weak and sleepy.

Once more Barry seemed to know just what to do. He didn't run back to the monastery this time. He lay down beside the little girl instead. He half covered her with his warm, furry body. And he began to lick her face with his big, rough tongue.

At first the girl didn't move. But slowly as she grew warmer she began to stir. She snuggled under Barry's belly. And she opened her eyes.

She wasn't frightened. She knew right away the big dog was a friend. She continued to snuggle close to his side — and slowly his warmth woke her up. But she was still too weak to stand.

Barry looked around. It was very cold now. But when the sun went down it would be much, much colder.

Barry tugged at the girl's coat. He stood up. He lay down beside her again. It was as if he were telling her something. And maybe he was. Because now the little girl threw one leg around Barry's body. She wrappped her arms around his furry neck. And a few minutes later the St Bernard padded slowly into the courtyard of the monastery with the little girl riding on his back!

Stories like this soon made Barry famous on both sides of the mountains. Barry just went on doing his job. He did it for more than twelve years. And during that time he helped save the lives of 42 people.

But the work was hard and the weather was harsh. Soon after Barry's twelfth birthday the monks noticed that the dog was growing stiff and slow.

Most old dogs were sent to homes in the

warmer valleys below. But the monks couldn't bear to part with Barry. So he stayed at the monastery for several more years.

Then winter came once more. One wild and stormy night Barry was sleeping by the fire. There was a lull in the storm. The monks heard nothing. But Barry's ears were still sharp. Suddenly he was wide awake. He moved to the door and began to whine.

The monks thought he wanted to go into the courtyard. But when they opened the door Barry dashed away into the night.

Not far away Barry found what he was looking for — a man lying face downward in the snow. The man must have shouted a few minutes before. But now he lay very still with his eyes closed.

Barry bent over him. The man rolled over. He half opened his eyes. And what he saw made him scream. A big, dim shape was looming over him! "It's a wolf!" the man thought. With the last of his strength he pulled out his knife — and stuck it deep into Barry's side. Then he fainted again.

The old dog was badly wounded. But he

still had a job to do. Somehow Barry got back to the monastery. He sank to the ground. And the monks, lanterns held high, followed the paw prints — and drops of blood — back to the man.

They were in time to save the man's life. But no one in the monastery was happy that night. The monks took turns looking after Barry. At first they thought he would surely die. But finally he grew a little stronger.

Barry grew stronger, but he was never really well again. And he died a few months later.

The monks and the big St Bernards still live in the high mountains of Switzerland. But life at the monastery is very different now. Far below, a tunnel goes through the mountain. And a safe road has been built through the pass nearby.

So the dogs are no longer needed for rescue work. But Barry has not been forgotten. Every few years, when an especially lively and intelligent pup is born at the monastery, he is always named Barry.

5

Balto – the dog who saved an Alaskan town

"THIS IS NOME, ALASKA. REPEAT.
THIS IS NOME, ALASKA. WE NEED HELP.
FAST . . . "

A man bent over the machine in the Nome telegraph office. Again and again he pressed down the signal key. *Click-click-clack . . . Clack-click-clack . . .* He was sending a message to the town of Anchorage, Alaska, 500 kilometres to the south.

Click-click-clack . . . Clack-click-clack . . . The Anchorage telegraph operator wrote down the message. The news was very bad.

A terrible sickness had broken out in the Nome area — a disease called diphtheria. Some people had already died of it. Many more would die if they weren't treated soon.

There was no medicine to treat diphtheria in Nome. The medicine they needed would have to come from Anchorage — 500 kilometres away — through a wild wind and snow storm. The storm was so bad that aeroplanes couldn't fly through it. Trains couldn't get through it either. Nome was very near the sea, but the sea was frozen solid. And the road from the south was completely blocked by deep drifts of snow.

There was only one way to get the medicine from Anchorage to Nome — by dogsled.

The medicine was packed in a box and sent north by train — as far as the train could go on the snowy tracks. It was still more than 375 kilometres to Nome. From now on teams of dogs would have to take it the rest of the way.

The teams were ready. The first team pushed north through the storm to a little town. There a second team was waiting. It went to another small town where a third team was ready to take the medicine on north.

At first the teams managed to go many miles before they grew tired. But the storm was growing worse by the minute. Finally Charlie Olson's team staggered into the little village of Bluff — 40 kilometres south of

Nome. They had only gone 15 kilometres, yet Olson and the dogs were almost frozen and completely worn out.

Gunnar Kasson and his team were waiting in Bluff. The wind screamed through the little town. The snow was piling up deeper and deeper on the ground. It was 30 degrees *below* zero Fahrenheit outside now. And the temperature was falling fast.

"It's no use trying to go out in *that*," Charlie Olson said. "I almost didn't make it. You and the dogs will freeze solid before you get half way."

But Kasson knew how important the medicine was. He knew that hundreds — maybe thousands — of people would die if they didn't get the medicine soon. Besides, he knew he didn't have to go all the way. Another team was waiting 30 kilometres north in the little village of Safety. That team would take the medicine the last 10 kilometres to Nome.

Quickly Gunnar Kasson hitched up his team of dogs. And at the head of the long line he put his lead dog, Balto.

Balto was a mixed-breed. He was half Eskimo dog — and half wolf. Many dogs who are part wolf never become tame. They never learn to trust people — or obey them either. Balto was different. He was a gentle dog who obeyed orders quickly. He also knew how to think for himself.

Usually Gunnar Kasson guided the dogs. He told them where to go. Now he couldn't even see his hand in front of his face. So everything was up to Balto. The big black dog would have to find the trail by smell. Then he'd have to stay on it no matter what happened.

Gunnar Kasson climbed on to the back of the sled. He cracked his whip in the air. "*Mush!*" he cried. "*Move out!*"

The first part of the trail to Nome led across the sea ice. This ice wasn't anything like the ice on a small pond or lake. It seemed much more *alive*. And no wonder. The water *under* the ice was moving up and down because of the storm. So the ice was moving up and down too. Up and down, up and down it went, like a roller coaster.

In some places the ice was as smooth as polished marble and as slippery as glass. Dogs are usually sure-footed. But they slipped and skidded across this ice. So did the sled.

And sometimes the ice came to sharp points — points that dug deep into the dogs' paws.

Worst of all were the places where the ice was bumpy — so bumpy that the sled turned over again and again. Each time it turned over the other dogs began to bark and snap at each other. But Balto always stood quietly while Kasson set the sled upright again. Balto was calm, so the other dogs grew calmer too.

The team had been moving across the ice for hours. Suddenly there was a loud *cracking*

sound — like a gun going off. Kasson knew that sound. It was the sound of ice breaking. Somewhere not far ahead the ice had split apart. If the team kept going straight they would run right into the freezing water — and drown.

Balto heard the ice crack too. He slowed for a moment. Then he turned left. He headed straight out to sea. He went for a long time. Then he turned right once more.

Balto was leading the team *around* the icy water. Finally he gave a sharp bark and turned north. He had found the trail to Nome again.

Soon the trail left the sea ice. From now on it was over land. Things should have been easier. They weren't. The snow was falling thick and fast. In some places the wind swept most of it off the trail. But in other places the snow drifts came up almost over the dogs' heads. And the wind was blowing harder and harder. It sent bits of icy snow straight into Kasson's eyes. "I might as well have been blind," he said. "I couldn't even *guess* where we were."

And the dogs were so tired! Again and again they tried to stop. They wanted to lie down and go to sleep in the snow. Balto was just as tired. But he would not stop. He kept on pulling — and the other dogs had to follow behind.

Now something else began to worry Gunnar Kasson. They had been travelling for about fourteen hours. Surely they should have reached the town of Safety in fourteen hours. Kasson went on for another hour. Then he knew. Somehow they had missed the town in the storm. They must have passed right by the new dog team!

Kasson knew they couldn't stop and wait for the storm to die down. He and the dogs would freeze if they did. They couldn't go back to Bluff either. They had come too far. There was only one thing to do now. Pray . . . and push on to Nome.

Later Gunnar Kasson said he couldn't remember those last kiolmetres very well. Each one was a nightmare of howling wind and swirling snow and bitter cold. But somehow — with Balto leading slowly and steadily —. they made it! At 5.30 in the morning of February 2nd 1925 — after twenty hours on the trail — the team limped into Nome!

The whole town was waiting for the medicine! They gathered around Gunnar Kasson. They shook his hand and pounded him on the back. "How can we ever thank you?" one woman cried.

Gunnar Kasson shook his head. Then he sank to his knees beside Balto. He began to pull long splinters of ice from the dog's paws. "Balto, what a dog!" he said. "I've been in Alaska for twenty years and this was the toughest trip I've ever made. But Balto, *he* brought us through."

Many newspaper and magazine stories were written about Balto. His picture was printed on postcards and in books. And today, on a grassy hill in New York City's Central Park, there is a life-sized statue of Balto — the dog who saved Nome.

6

Justin Morgan – the biggest little horse of all

Justin Morgan walked along a dirt road in Massachusetts. He was too poor to own a horse. This was two hundred years ago, so he had to walk wherever he wanted to go. Justin had come all the way from Vermont to collect some money a man owed him.

But when he got there the man said, "If you want money you'll just have to wait. I can give you something else though." He pointed to two horses in a field nearby.

Justin was a teacher. He didn't need a horse. And the man owed him much more money than Justin would get from selling those two horses. But he had come a long way. Two horses were better than nothing. Finally Justin nodded and started home with the horses.

One horse was big and powerful-looking. Justin could sell him. But he shook his head when he looked at the other horse — a colt he named

Figure. Figure was only fourteen hands high (a hand is four inches or about ten centimetres). That *wasn't* very big for a horse. "He's probably worth nothing at all," Justin thought.

Figure had run wild for two years. His coat was covered with mud and dust. Justin could hardly tell what colour he was. So when he reached home, Justin Morgan washed the little horse. He picked all the burrs out of his mane and tail. Then he brushed and combed him all over until his coat gleamed in the sun.

"Why, he's *handsome*!" Justin's daughter Emily cried.

It was true. The horse's legs and ears were a shiny black. The rest of his coat was a nice reddish-brown. His mane and tail were thick and long. His back was straight and his muscles firm and strong.

Figure had never been trained. But he learned quickly. Soon he was pulling carriages and wagons. He was so gentle that even the youngest child could ride him.

And he was clever. "Sometimes I think that horse knows what I'm thinking before I do myself," Justin said.

Figure was strong too. He could carry a rider or pull a wagon all day — and never seem to tire. Best of all, he was always willing to do whatever was asked of him.

Justin Morgan was proud of Figure. But he was very poor. He couldn't afford to keep a horse. He didn't want to sell him either. Maybe he could rent him to someone.

Justin went to a neighbour named Robert Evans. "I hear you need a horse," he said. "What about renting mine?"

Mr Evans had heard good things about Figure, but still he said, "That horse of yours is too small — and the work I do is very hard. What I need is a really *big* horse."

Justin smiled and said, "Try him." So for fifteen dollars a year Figure was rented to Robert Evans. Soon Mr Evans knew what a good bargain he'd made.

Two hundred years ago horses did the work that farm machines and cars do today. They were never treated like pets. They were work animals — that was all.

Every day Evans and Figure went to work. From dawn until dark they hauled heavy logs out of the woods. They pulled big stumps and rocks from the ground. It was hard, hard work — but Figure was always willing.

One evening Robert Evans and Figure passed a saw-mill on their way home. Men and horses were standing in the clearing in front of the mill. A huge pine log lay on the ground more than 50 metres from the saw-mill.

"What's going on?" Robert Evans called out. A man explained. One horse after another had tried to drag the log to the mill. But none had been able to move it more than a few centimetres.

Robert Evans walked over to the log. He looked at it from one side — and then the other. "Why, Figure can do it," he said. Everyone looked at Justin Morgan's horse. Some began to laugh. "*That* horse?" one man said. "Why, horses almost twice his size couldn't move that log."

"I say Figure can do it," he said again. "And I say he can do it in three pulls — or less."

He snapped one end of a heavy chain to

Figure's harness. He wrapped the other end around the log Then he patted Figure on the shoulder. "All right, boy," he said quietly. "It's just another log — only bigger."

Then "Giddap!" he cried. Figure tensed. He leaned forward. His hoofs dug into the ground. Every muscle in his body strained. He was pulling as hard as he could. And nothing was happening.

Then somehow he pulled just a little bit harder — and the log moved! At first only a

centimetre. Then three centimetres. Then a metre! Slowly Figure dragged the log to the middle of the clearing.

"Whoa, boy," Robert Evans said. For a few minutes the little horse rested. Then "Come on," said Robert Evans. "Time to work some more."

Once more Figure strained forward. Once more the log began to move slowly and steadily — right up to the mill.

Everyone began to talk at once. "What a horse!" one man said. "Why, that Morgan horse is the *biggest* little horse I've ever seen!"

A few weeks later — at the end of a hard day's work — Robert Evans and Figure passed a country shop where a group of men were racing their horses.

"Want to try your horse, Evans?" someone called.

Robert Evans nodded. "I might."

"Oh, come on," one of the men said. "I know Morgan's horse can pull logs. But his legs are too short for racing."

"I'm sure he can do as well as the next one," Evans said. "I think I'd like to try."

Figure had never been in a race. Still, he seemed to sense that something exciting was about to happen. He began to prance. Then — "One-two-three . . . Go!" someone shouted.

Figure took the lead straight away! The race wasn't over, though. The other horses had much longer legs. Surely they would catch up before he got to the end. But Figure held his lead. He won by four times the length of his own body.

Figure ran in many races after that, and he won most of them too. Even thoroughbreds — horses specially bred for speed — were usually no match for the tough little Morgan horse.

One day Justin Morgan went to see Robert Evans. "I need money badly," he said. "The fifteen dollars rent you pay for Figure each year is just not enough. I hate to do it — but I have to sell the horse." So both men watched sadly as Figure was led away.

Soon after that Justin Morgan became ill. His fever rose and his cough grew worse and worse. One day he lay in bed talking to a

friend. "I know I am dying," he said. "And soon no one will know I've been alive. No one will remember my name."

How wrong he was! Already many people were calling Figure by Justin Morgan's name. Before long everyone would be thinking of the *horse* as Justin Morgan.

People talked about the horse Justin Morgan because they had noticed something very unusual. The foals of Justin Morgan all looked like him. It didn't matter what their mother looked like. They all had his same intelligent eyes. They all had his sturdy legs and strong muscles. And they grew up to *be* like him too. They were all gentle yet spirited, strong and fast and eager to work.

People wanted horses with these qualities. So they mated their own horses to the first Justin Morgan and then to his children and grandchildren and great-grandchildren.

Soon Morgan horses were carrying the mail. They were taking Americans westward — all the way to California. They were fighting in wars and working on farms. They became fire horses and police horses and racing horses and riding horses. And so a new breed of horse was born.

7

Misty – the pony who helped save a whole herd

It's Pony Penning Day!

Fishermen and chicken farmers who live on the island of Chincoteague become cowboys for a day. Early in the morning they cross the narrow channel of water that separates their island from the neighbouring island of Assateague.

There — more than eight kilometres off the coast of Virginia — live hundreds of wild ponies. No one knows how they got there. But they have roamed free on the island for hundreds of years.

The wild ponies are rounded up and driven into the water and across the channel to Chincoteague. Then the whole herd — almost two hundred stallions and mares and foals of all ages — gallops down the main street of town to the fairgrounds.

Each year thousands of people from all

over America go to Chincoteague on Pony Penning Day. They come to play games and watch horse races and go on all sorts of fair rides. However, mainly they go to look at the wild ponies. And some also go to buy one. Every year many of the half-grown ponies are sold. The rest are driven back to Assateague. (If some of the ponies weren't sold every year, there would soon be too many on the island — and not enough food for any of them to eat.)

Twenty-five thousand people went to Pony Penning Day in the summer of 1946. One was a writer named Marguerite Henry. Pony Penning Day was almost over when Mrs Henry saw a mare standing a little apart from the other ponies. Lying by the mare's side was a tiny foal.

The foal's eyes were bright brown with long gold eyelashes. Around one eye was a big gold patch. It made the little horse look like a happy clown!

Mrs Henry knew she had to own this foal. But the mare and foal had already been sold to a man who lived on Chincoteague — a man everyone called Grandpa Beebe.

Grandpa didn't want to sell the pony. "She's only a week old. That's far too young to leave her mother. Take another," he said.

But Marguerite Henry knew that *this* was the foal she had to have. "I *need* her," she begged. "I'm a writer. I want to build a book around an Assateague pony. And somehow I know it will be a better book if this pony is with me while I'm writing it."

"Well . . ." Grandpa Beebe scratched his ear. "If you let her stay here for a few months — until she's old enough to leave her mother . . ."

"Of course!" Marguerite Henry agreed quickly. Then she made Grandpa Beebe a promise. "When she's old enough to be a mother herself, I'll send her back to you.

Then her babies will be real Assateague ponies too."

Marguerite Henry went home and began to write her book — and a few months later the half-grown pony arrived in Illinois. Mrs Henry named her Misty.

A few of the neighbourhood children came to see Misty. But no one else knew about the little horse who had come from so far away.

Then the book was finished. It was called *Misty of Chincoteague* — and from the beginning it was huge success. The book was full of adventures — some of them true and some made up.

Now many people knew about Misty. Everyone wanted to see the little pony. She was asked to horse shows. She visited schools and libraries and book shops. She went to all kinds of parties. Finally Marguerite Henry had to buy a special diary — just to write down all of Misty's invitations!

Misty loved those trips. She liked to show off. And she learned some tricks. She had a little blue stool. She learned to put her front hoofs up on it and bow from left to right. She

also learned to shake "hands" with her right or left hoof. Soon she was offering a hoof to almost everyone in sight!

Marguerite Henry had made a promise to Grandpa Beebe. She had promised to send Misty back to Chincoteague when she was old enough to be a mother. But Mrs Henry loved Misty so much! Somehow the years kept slipping by and Misty was still in Illinois.

Finally Mrs Henry knew it was time — no, it was past time — to send Misty back to her first home. "Don't worry," she said to the many children who came to say goodbye. "I *know* Misty will be happy to be returning home."

And she was. Misty spent her days running through the pine woods and salty meadows with Grandpa Beebe's other ponies. And about a year later her first foal was born. All across the country, radio and television stations carried the good news about the new mother and her little colt named Phantom Wings.

Anyone who had not heard of Misty before soon found out who she was. A film was made of the book *Misty of Chincoteague*. Misty didn't play herself in the film, of course. It was about a very young pony and Misty was full grown now. But she played one of the other wild horses in the film. When she wasn't acting she spent a lot of time shaking hands with anyone who happened to be nearby.

Time passed happily for Misty. Then early one morning 1962, clouds rolled across the sky. Throughout the day it grew darker and darker. An icy cold wind blew from the north. By evening a freezing rain was falling.

Most people weren't worried at first — they were used to stormy weather. But all night long the wind and rain grew worse. Early next morning the people of Chincoteague looked out of their windows — and saw water everywhere! It was beginning to lap against the sides of their homes. And it was still rising!

Misty was about to have another foal. By mid-morning water was flowing across the floor of her stable. The water was full of mud and sand and bits of strange things. First it slapped against her hoofs. Then centimetre by centimetre it started to creep up her legs. Misty gave a nervous whinny.

All day people sat by their radios and listened as the news grew worse. The causeway to the mainland was under water. The people of Chincoteague were cut off. They were trapped on a small piece of land ten kilometres out in the raging sea!

Late in the afternoon the government said everyone would have to leave. Helicopters would take them to safe places on the mainland.

But what about Misty? There was no room in the helicopters for animals. The Beebes did the only thing they could. They led Misty across the watery back garden, up the porch steps, and into their kitchen. The house was on a small hill, so the floor was still dry. They piled hay in a corner and filled the big sink with water. They dumped all the vegetables in the refrigerator on the floor. Then they gave her one last pat and left.

The storm raged for four more days. Then the wind began to die down. The rain stopped and the water began to go down. The causeway to the island was above water once more. The people of Chincoteague could go home.

But to what? The storm had done terrible damage. Some houses leaned crazily to one side. Others weren't there — they'd been swept out to sea. Cars and vans had been tossed about like toys. Boats had been lifted out of the water and thrown on to the land.

But Misty was fine. She'd eaten all the hay and vegetables. She'd drunk all the water. Then — somehow — she had opened the refrigerator door and tipped over a full bottle of her favourite treat — molasses.

Early the next morning Misty gave birth to a little tan-and-white daughter. It had been hard to name Misty's first foal. Everyone had had a different idea. But there was no trouble naming this fuzzy little filly. She was Stormy, of course!

As soon as things had been cleaned up, a little group of men rowed over to Assateague. Some of the ponies there had reached higher land. But more than half the herd had been swept out to sea. Would there ever be another Pony Penning Day — with so few of the wild horses left?

Then someone had an idea. Suppose the

people of Chincoteague brought back some of the ponies — those that had been sold over the years? These ponies would have foals and build up the herd once more. It was a good idea — but where would they get the money to buy the ponies?

Then one of the men who had made the film about Misty called the mayor of Chincoteague. He wanted to know how everyone was after the storm. The mayor told him about their problem.

"What if we show the film again?" the man said. "We'll send it to every cinema that wants it. And all the money it makes will go towards buying back the ponies."

It sounded wonderful. But so many children had just seen the film. Would they go and see it again, so soon? What if Misty and Stormy went *with* the film . . . . Surely the boys and girls would come then!

The first cinema that Misty and Stormy visted was in Richmond, Virginia. By ten o'clock the big cinema was packed.

"We want Misty! We want Stormy!" the boys and girls yelled. A man came down the centre aisle leading Misty and her foal. When they reached the steps to the stage, Misty trotted right up them. But Stormy stopped. Misty turned and whinnied softly. "Come along," she seemed to be saying. "There is nothing to be afraid of." Stormy stood for a moment more. Then she wobbled up the steps too.

Misty's special blue stool was on the stage. As soon as she saw it she walked over and climbed up on it. Then she bowed from left to right. Everyone began to clap and whistle and yell. Misty looked back at the boys and girls and slowly blinked her eyes.

For three months mother and daughter went from town to town and cinema to cinema. Misty stood on her stool and shook hands with long lines of boys and girls. Stormy played happily on all the different stages. Sometimes mother and daughter stood nose to nose, making soft sounds to one another. As one man said when he saw them, "Those two are *born* actors!"

When the tour was over, enough money had been raised to buy back about fifty ponies. Misty and Stormy — along with boys and girls all across America — had saved the wild herd of Assateague.

8

Brighty – the donkey who belonged to himself

"The buds are out on the aspens," Uncle Jim thought. "And yesterday I saw some ground squirrels. Brighty's sure to be coming up his trail any day now."

Brighty didn't belong to Uncle Jim Owens. He didn't belong to anyone — except himself. All donkeys are very independent, but Brighty was more independent than most.

Brighty wasn't a wild donkey. He wasn't tame either. No one knew where he came from. He spent half his winters in the Grand Canyon, where it was always warm. Sometimes while he was there, he helped an old miner by carrying his tools. But more often Brighty just played. He rolled on his back. He ran in the shallow creek, splashing water everywhere. Often he just sat and brayed at the top of his lungs.

Brighty always did just as he pleased. And now that spring had come, it pleased Brighty to climb the steep canyon to his cool summer home on the North Rim.

During the summer Brighty often visited Uncle Jim. But he didn't live with him. Brighty's special home was a cave near the edge of the canyon. The cave was always dim inside. Its floor was covered with soft ferns. And near the back wall was a deep pool of cool water.

One night as Brighty slept, a shape came creeping through the dark. It peered into the cave — its eyes gleaming like gold.

It was a hungry mountain lion! For a moment the lion stood staring at Brighty. Then it crouched — and sprang towards the donkey. The lion was probably aiming to sink his claws into Brighty's neck — and that would have been the end of Brighty. But in the dark the lion missed. Not by much, but enough. Those terrible claws slashed down Brighty's front legs instead.

Brighty jumped to his feet. He kicked back hard with his little hoofs. But the lion leapt aside. Once more it crouched — and this time it sprang on to Brighty's back!

Brighty tore round and round the cave, trying to shake off the snarling cat. Then he fell to the ground and began rolling over and over. But the lion wouldn't let go.

As Brighty rolled, he moved closer and closer to the pool. At last he rolled into the water — pinning the lion underneath him. The lion still fought wildly, trying to keep its head above water. But Brighty's body held it down. Two minutes, three minutes, then four

minutes passed. Finally the cat's claws loosened. Brighty staggered out of the water and fell to the floor of the cave.

That's where Uncle Jim Owens found him the next day. He gasped as he stepped inside the cave. The dead lion lay in the pool. And Brighty was on his side, his eyes were closed and his legs were covered in blood.

Uncle Jim put his hand on Brighty's chest. The donkey's heart was still beating strongly. Quickly the man set to work. He gathered big wads of gooey pine tar from a nearby tree and spread it all over Brighty's legs.

The soothing salve seemed to make Brighty feel better almost at once. He struggled to his knees. Swaying, he got to his feet. Then he began to do what any hurt animal does — he began to lick his wounds.

"You can't do that, fella," Uncle Jim said. "You'll take off all the pine tar." But Brighty just carried on licking.

Uncle Jim sighed. If only he had some kind of bandage. Then Brighty wouldn't be able to get at the wounds.

Suddenly Uncle Jim had a crazy idea. He

took out his penknife and cut off his left trouser leg at the knee. Then he cut off the right one. He stepped out of the two pieces of cloth and pulled them up Brighty's front legs. The two bottom halves of Uncle Jim's trousers covered Brighty right up to his chest.

But what could he use to keep the cloth up? Uncle Jim chuckled. He took off his bright red braces and laid them across Brighty's back. Finally he clipped the braces to the tops of the cloth legs.

Now each of them — the man and the donkey — was wearing half a pair of trousers. "And pretty silly we look too!" said Uncle Jim.

Brighty lived at Uncle Jim's ranch for the next few weeks. Every evening the old man slipped Brighty's trousers off and rubbed his legs with soothing salve. Then he slipped the trousers back on again.

One evening Uncle Jim came out of his house as usual. But he didn't collect any tar. Instead he pulled off Brighty's trousers and threw them away. "You're all healed now," he told the donkey. "You don't need those trousers any more." Uncle Jim gave Brighty a slap on his rump. "So go on. You're free to go wherever you want to now!"

Brighty dashed round and round in a big circle. And HEEEE-HAWWWW! — the sound of his happy bray filled the air.

But Brighty didn't leave the ranch. The summer days passed and he never even visited his cave. Soon it was autumn. Every day grew colder on the high North Rim. It was long past time for Brighty to leave for his winter home deep in the Grand Canyon.

Often Brighty went to the edge of the canyon. He stood there for hours — staring down. But still he didn't leave.

Uncle Jim was getting more and more worried. He had healed Brighty's legs. Had he somehow tamed his free spirit too?

Then one day Brighty began to move down the trail — very, very slowly. As Uncle Jim watched, Brighty stopped and turned. He walked on a little more. And stopped again. Uncle Jim knew he could call, "Brighty, come back!" and the grateful animal would probably obey. But the man didn't make a sound. He just watched as Brighty moved down into the canyon. At last he was out of sight.

Uncle Jim would miss his friend. But he was happy all the same. For he knew that Brighty would remain a free donkey for the rest of his life.

So every winter Brighty lived deep in the canyon. Every summer he spent on the North Rim. And always he came and went the same way.

In those days — almost a hundred years ago — very few people tried to get down to the bottom of the Grand Canyon. Its sides were too steep and there were no trails. Little by little, Brighty's hoofs wore a path — a path people began calling Bright Angel Trail.

More and more people began to use Brighty's path — teachers and students and writers, miners and explorers and scientists. Many tourists came too. They all wanted to see what lay at the bottom of the Grand Canyon.

Sometimes Brighty stayed with these people for a while. When he felt like it he even worked for them. Often he gave children rides on his back. Sometimes three or four boys and girls would climb on at the same time. And Brighty would amble from place to place. When he got tired or bored he just walked under a low branch of a tree. It was his way of saying, "Time to get off now."

One morning in the winter of 1921 Brighty was awakened by a sound like thunder — only much louder. For a few minutes everything was quiet. Then the strange sound came again.

Brighty followed the sound to the bank of the Colorado River. There he blinked with surprise. Men were moving about everywhere. Suddenly the sound came once more. And big chunks of stone flew into the air. The men were blowing holes in the rock with dynamite.

The Colorado River flows down the middle of the Grand Canyon. It is only 122 metres wide. But it cuts the canyon in half. The men were building a bridge across the river — a bridge to link the two halves of the canyon at last.

Brighty sat down to watch. "Hey! You must be Brighty," one of the workers called after a while. "Why don't you come and help?"

Brighty walked over. And before long he was carrying tools and equipment . Often he carried heavy bags of sand for making cement. Brighty didn't work every day, of course. Just when he felt like it.

Slowly the bridge took shape. When it was

finished many important people gathered for the Opening Day Ceremony. The Governor of Colorado made a grand speech. Then it was time for the first person to cross the bridge.

"I say Brighty should be the first one across," someone called out. "It's *his* trail that helped open up the canyon for the rest of us."

"Besides," another man added, " Brighty is the only true citizen of the Grand Canyon here today."

But *would* Brighty cross the bridge? Donkeys don't like to do dangerous things. Certainly he would never go alone. Uncle Jim stepped forward. "I'll go with Brighty," he said.

They walked up to the bridge. At the edge, Brighty stopped in his tracks. The bridge was very long and narrow — and it was *swaying* in the wind.

Brighty's ears went back. He began to shake. Uncle Jim knew these signs well. Brighty was about to run away.

"Trust me, Brighty," Uncle Jim said

quietly. "We'll be across in no time at all."

Uncle Jim put one of his own big feet on the bridge. He reached down and placed one of Brighty's tiny hoofs beside it. Brighty was still shaking. But he didn't bolt. Uncle Jim put his other foot on the bridge. He reached down again — and both Brighty's front hoofs were on the bridge too.

Now — with his hand on Brighty's shoulder — Uncle Jim began to walk. And so did Brighty. Metre by metre they walked across the bridge until they were safe on the other side!

The men cheered wildly. HEE-HAWWWWW! Brighty brayed back.

Brighty's world was bigger now. He could wander on both sides of the Grand Canyon. But in the spring he always returned to his friends on the North Rim.

Then one spring Brighty didn't appear. He was never to be seen again. No one really knows what happened. Some people say Brighty was shot by an outlaw who was hiding in the canyon. But others say this isn't true. They say that Brighty lived a good long life in the Grand Canyon of Colorado. And finally he just died of old age. He died —as he had lived — a free donkey to the last.

9

Clever Hans – the horse who knew all the answers

Hans lived with his owner, Mr von Osten, in Berlin, Germany. One day Mr von Osten invited some friends to his house. He led them to a courtyard where the horse was waiting quietly. "Are you ready, Hans?" he asked.

And the horse nodded!

"How much is four plus three?" Mr von Osten asked. Hans raised his right foreleg and began to tap his hoof on the old stone floor of the courtyard. "One, two, three," he tapped, "four, five, six, seven" — and stopped.

Everyone began to talk at once. Mr von Osten just smiled — and asked another question.

"It's twelve-thirty now," he said to the horse. "How many minutes must pass before it will be one o'clock?" Quickly Hans tapped *thirty*.

Next Mr von Osten spread out six squares

of cloth. Each was a different colour. "Pick up the green one," he ordered. Hans walked over and stopped in front of the green square. He picked it up in his teeth and carried it back to his master.

Then Mr von Osten looked around at his friends. "There is a lady here," he told Hans, "who is wearing a hat with pink flowers on it. Will you point her out for the rest of us?" The woman was small — and she was standing behind several other people. But still Hans managed to find her.

For the next hour Mr von Osten asked questions — and Hans answered them. He was right almost every time.

Finally Mr von Osten said, "That's enough for today. But Hans will be here tomorrow to answer more questions."

All this happened before there was any radio or television and people were eager for any kind of entertainment. Slowly word of the horse and what he could do spread through Berlin, then all of Germany — and then even into other countries. More and more people came to the von Osten courtyard to see the wonder horse perform.

Clever Hans never disappointed his audience. He could solve hard arithmetic problems. "How much is nine times sixty-eight?" Mr von Osten once asked Hans. It took the horse quite a while to tap the right answer — 612!

Almost every day Hans showed his eager audiences some new talent. He could tell all sorts of things apart — even if they were almost the same size or shade or shape. Hans could also give the right answer when asked the time. And the days and weeks and months of the year.

One day Mr von Osten stretched a rope across the courtyard. On the rope he hung a number of cards. On each card a word was printed. "Where is the card thats reads 'hello'?" he asked. Hans walked up to the HELLO card and nudged it with his nose. "And which card reads 'Germany'?" Hans picked the correct card again. Finally Mr von Osten asked, "And which is your own special card?" Hans walked up to the card that said HANS and gave it a really hard nudge.

"The only thing that horse can't do is talk," one man said. But other people said Hans did that too — with his hoof.

Hans had one talent that amazed people more than all the rest. Mr von Osten could stand in front of the horse and just *think* of a question. He didn't move his lips or make the slightest sound. Yet Hans would answer the question anyway. So, Clever Hans could read his master's mind too!

But not everyone agreed that Hans was a

real thinking horse. Paul Bushe had worked with circus animals nearly all his life. "I know all the tricks," he bragged. "Nobody can fool me — no matter how smart he thinks he is." He thought Mr von Osten was sending Hans signals — signals that told the horse exactly what to do.

Mr Bushe wanted to find those hidden signals. So he paid a surprise visit to the von Osten courtyard. With him were five other men. He told Mr von Osten that they were there to study him while he worked with Hans. One man would stare at his head. Another would watch his left arm. A third would watch his right. The last two men would watch one leg each.

Mr von Osten nodded grimly. He knew that the circus trainer was calling him a liar and a cheat to his face. "And what will *you* watch?" he asked.

"Oh, I shall watch *everything*," Paul Bushe answered grandly.

Mr von Osten began asking questions — and Hans as usual answered most of them correctly. All the time the six men watched.

They watched so hard one man said he almost forgot to breathe.

Finally Mr Bushe threw up his hands. "Forgive me," he said to Mr von Osten. "I still find it hard to believe . . . but I was wrong. No signals have passed between you and the horse. Not one. I am the greatest circus trainer in Germany — and I am going to tell the world that clever Hans is, indeed, a thinking horse. As a matter of fact, he can think better than most people I know!"

A few weeks later another man came to Mr von Osten's courtyard. Carl Shillings was a famous explorer. For many years he had lived in faraway lands. "I have never seen Clever Hans — and he's never seen me," he said to Mr von Osten. "There is no way I could have worked out to send him signals. Will you let *me* question the horse?"

"Of course I will," Mr von Osten said. "I will even leave the courtyard if you wish. Then you can work with Hans all by yourself."

As soon as he was alone Mr Shillings began to ask Hans questions. At first the horse seemed confused. He pranced a little and looked around the courtyard. But soon he settled down and began to answer Mr Shillings' questions.

He made a few mistakes, but before long he was giving one right answer after another. So a perfect stranger could ask Hans questions too — a man who could not possibly be part of any plan to fool people. Surely this was final proof that Clever Hans was a true thinking horse!

But still a few people had questions. One of these was a scientist named Oskar Pfungst. Other people had studied Hans for a few hours, or a few days. Professor Pfungst decided he would work for as long as it took to finally solve the mystery of Clever Hans.

First Professor Pfungst started out asking questions, just as other people had done. And Hans answered easily. Then one day the scientist thought of something new. He asked Hans a question that was different in one important way from all the other questions the big horse had ever been asked. He asked the horse a question *he didn't know the answer to*

himself. "How far is it from Berlin to London?" he asked.

Poor Hans! He tried again and again to answer that question. But he couldn't do it. The Professor grew more and more excited. He kept asking questions. When he asked a question he knew the answer to, Hans knew the answer. When he asked a question that he didn't know the answer to, Hans didn't either.

Before the day was over, Professor Pfungst knew that Hans couldn't really add or subtract or multiply or divide. He couldn't tell colours or coins or playing cards apart. He couldn't read or tell the time. Hans wasn't a thinking horse at all. He only "knew" as much as the person who was questioning him — and no more.

That meant that the person questioning Hans *was* signalling to him. But how? Even the Professor himself must be sending signals — but he had no idea how he was doing it.

Day after day Professor Pfungst continued to ask Hans questions. He watched as many other people questioned the horse. And little by little he began to understand.

Most trained animals can follow signals — like a hand movement or a change in the tone of voice. But none of these planned signals had ever been used with Hans. No, Professor Pfungst announced, people who questioned Hans were signalling to Hans even though they did not mean to.

First the person aked Hans a question — and naturally he grew a little tense, a little nervous, as he waited for the horse's answer. When this happened many tiny body changes began to take place — changes the person wasn't trying to make at all. A muscle might quiver in his ear. He might swallow a few more times than usual. His lips might tighten. Or one of his eyebrows would give the slightest twitch. All these were signs of tension. And these signs told Hans to start giving his answers.

Suppose the person had asked Hans how much five plus five is. With each tap of Hans's hoof, the person got more and more tense. 1—2—3—4—5—6—7—8—9— Then, as Hans tapped 10, the person relaxed.

Now another whole group of tiny changes

began to take place. The person might take a slightly deeper breath — or begin to breathe more slowly. His lips might open a little. His eyelids might droop. His skin might even grow a bit pinker. All these are tiny signs of relaxation. And put together they told Hans to stop.

When someone wanted Hans to nod *yes*, he couldn't help making some kind of upward motion himself. And when someone wanted Hans to walk over to something — a person or perhaps a coloured cloth or ball — he couldn't help making some small movement in that direction. Hans would wander around until he happened to pass in front of what the person was thinking about. Then the person would relax — and Hans would stop. He had given the "right" answer again.

So Clever Hans couldn't really work out problems — not the way people do. Yet he was still a very special horse. He had puzzled one expert after another for a long, long time. He might not have read minds — but there was no doubt about it. He was one of the champion *muscle* readers of all time!

10

Pelorus Jack – the faithful dolphin

The country of New Zealand is made up of two main islands. Between them is a big body of water called Cook Strait. One summer day in 1888 a steamship was going through those waters, carrying passengers from one island to another. Suddenly a dolphin came to the top of the water. He swam with the ship for miles. Sometimes he swam by the side of the ship. Sometimes he swam in front of it. Then, with a flick of his tail, he was gone.

But the next day the dolphin was back. And the next, and the next — always swimming with one ship or another. But at the end of the day the dolphin would swim away. He would swim into a small inlet of water called Pelorus Bay. Before long, people began to call the dolphin Pelorus Jack.

The waters of Cook Strait were full of fast currents, jagged rocks, and even whirlpools. Some people thought that Pelorus Jack had decided to act as a pilot. They said he was showing the ship where it was safe to go.

"Nonsense!" other people said. "He's just having a good time."

Whatever the reason, more and more people began to go on the ships. They all wanted to see the dolphin. They would crowd close to the railings and peer out across the choppy water of Cook Strait. "Here comes Jack!" someone would cry as the dolphin raced towards the boat.

Jack became more and more famous. People wrote about him in magazines and newspapers. His picture was printed on postcards. A chocolate sweet was named after

him. And people came from far away to see the dolphin who swam with ships.

The sailors on these steamships had a special feeling for Jack. He brought them good luck, they said. As long as Pelorus Jack swam with their ship, nothing could go wrong. And nothing bad would ever happen to Jack either, the sailors said — not if they could help it.

But one day Jack was swimming with a ship named the *S.S. Penguin*. As usual, the railing high above the water was crowded with people laughing and talking and pointing at Jack. However, one young man was standing apart. When no one was looking he slowly raised a gun — and fired it at Jack!

The bullet whizzed through the air. It missed. But Jack dived deep in the water and sped away. From that day on, Pelorus Jack would not go near the *Penguin*.

Before long the sailors began to call the *Penguin* a bad-luck ship. One sailor would not work on her any more. "Jack won't have anything to do with her," he said. "Why should I?"

Now people began to worry about Jack. One man had already taken a shot at him. What was to stop another? Jack's many friends decided that a law should be passed to protect him. In 1904 the New Zealand government agreed. From then on it was against the law for anyone to harm Pelorus Jack in any way. This was the first law in history written especially to protect a dolphin.

For the next few years Pelorus Jack went on swimming with the ships. Then, in the summer of 1912, four Norwegian fishing boats sailed into Cook Strait. They were not supposed to fish for dolphins.

But a few days later Jack didn't show up. He didn't come around the next day, or the next. People on the ships would stare out over the water. They would think they saw something speeding towards them. "Here comes Jack!" they would cry. But their eyes — or their hearts — were playing tricks on them. Pelorus Jack was never seen again.

What had happened? Had Jack decided to go somewhere else? No one who knew the faithful dolphin could believe that. Maybe he had died of old age. Jack had been swimming with ships for twenty-four years. That is old for a dolphin.

But many of Jack's friends feared something else. They feared that one of the fishing boats had captured him — and boiled him down for oil!

Was this true? No one would ever know for sure. But a newspaper printed a story about Pelorus Jack's life. And it summed up everyone's feelings very well. The story ended: "If he is dead, more's the pity. If he has been slaughtered, more's the shame!"

11

Opo – the dolphin who loved people

Pelorus Jack loved ships. But he was a wild dolphin. In all the years he swam with ships he never let a person touch him.

Opo was different. She was a wild dolphin too. But she tamed herself. She liked to be close to people.

Opononi, New Zealand, was a quiet little town by the sea. Most of the men worked as fishermen. In the summer of 1955, they noticed that a strange sea animal was following their boats. At first the men thought it must be a shark. But the animal came closer and closer to the boats. And before long everyone could see it was a dolphin. One of the fishermen named her Opo — after the town.

At first Opo was shy, as many wild dolphins are. But she was curious too. Every day she swam closer to the boats. Finally, one of the fishermen reached out as far as he could with his oar, and scratched Opo with it.

She reared back in the water. But the oar must have felt good, for soon Opo came closer than ever before. Then she rolled over. The men had to laugh. For Opo was plainly saying "Scratch my belly, this time."

Opo swam alongside all kinds of boats. But she liked motorboats best. "She had a real weakness for the sound of an outboard motor," a fisherman said. "She would follow a motorboat just like a dog on a lead."

One evening Opo followed a motorboat all the way back to the town dock. From that day on she spent more and more time near the shore.

A scientist came to look at Opo. He said she was a young dolphin, who had probably lost her mother. That was why she was swimming alone. Opo might be an orphan, but she soon found a new family. The whole town of Opononi adopted the friendly dolphin.

Near the town dock was a sandy beach. Opo spent most of her time swimming there. At first she would dart away if anyone came too near. But before long she would swim with anyone who was gentle. She even let them touch her sometimes.

Opo liked children best of all. "I have seen her swimming among children almost begging to be petted," a woman remembers. Sometimes a child would stand in the water

with his legs apart. Then Opo would swim
under him, pick him up, and take him for a
short ride on her back.

One day someone gave Opo a beach ball.
She loved that ball! She balanced it on her
flippers. She bounced it high in the air. She
let it roll down her back and swatted it hard
with her tail.

The townspeople often stopped to watch Opo playing in the water. When she did something especially exciting they would cheer and clap. Then Opo would leap high in the air again and again. Opo, the once shy dolphin, had become a dolphin show-off. But she was careful never to leap when people were swimming nearby. She was always gentle with her human friends.

Before long news of Opo got around. More and more people began to make special trips to see the dolphin. Weekends were especially busy. There was only one hotel in town, and this was always fully booked. Every space in the nearby campsite was filled. And still more people came.

The one road that ran through town was often jammed with cars and lorries. The beach was packed with people. They all wanted to see Opo. Some people wanted to touch her so much they waded into the water with their clothes on.

The town was often very crowded. But the townspeople didn't mind. For this was a special kind of crowd. The gentle dolphin seemed to have the same effect on everyone. No one argued. No one got drunk. In the evening when it was too cold and dark to visit Opo, people sat around in small friendly groups and talked about her.

The townspeople of Opononi were happy to share Opo with others. But they had one worry. Someone had tried to shoot another dolphin, Pelorus Jack. What if that happened to Opo?

The people put up a sign on the edge of town — warning others not to shoot the dolphin. But a sign is only made of wood and words. What if words weren't enough? A law had been passed to protect Pelorus Jack. All over New Zealand people began to ask for a law to protect Opo.

In March 1956 a special law was passed to protect her. But on that very same day Opo did not come near the shore. She did not come to swim with the boats. She did not come to play with her human friends.

That first day no one worried very much. Opo had gone off on her own before, for a few hours at a time. But the next morning came — and still no Opo. Now people began to worry.

Four boats searched the harbour from end to end. But they found no sign of Opo. "She'll come back," the children said. *Please tell us she'll be back*, was what they really meant.

But Opo didn't come back — alive. The next morning a fisherman found her body caught on some rocks. Somehow she had stranded herself. No one ever knew why.

That evening Opo's body was brought back to the beach where she had played so happily. The next day she was buried beside the town hall. Her grave was covered with flowers. Almost everyone in town came to that funeral. Some stood sad and silent. Many were crying.

"I'll never forget her," one girl sobbed.

"Of course not," her mother answered. "None of us will."

And that was true. The friendly dolphin had come and made them happy. The people of Opononi would remember her forever.

12

Tuffy – the dolphin trained to save lives

Everyone knows about astronauts — the men who explore outer space. Now people are beginning to hear more and more about aquanauts, the men who explore space under water.

In the autumn of 1965 a group of aquanauts spent forty-five days under water near the coast of California. They were part of a project called Sealab II. One of the aquanauts looked a little different from the others. No wonder. He was a 136-kilogram dolphin named Tuffy.

Tuffy spent much of his time in a pen near the top of the water — so he could breathe. Home for the other aquanauts was a big metal capsule called Sealab which rested on the bottom of the ocean.

Every morning the human aquanauts put on their diving suits and left Sealab to swim in the water outside the capsule. They measured the underwater currents. They took pictures of the ocean floor. They put metal tags on the tails of some of the fish that swarmed around. They studied many different underwater plants.

Tuffy had jobs to do too. He had been trained to be a messenger. When he was working he wore a special harness. Waterproof bags could be hooked on to it. In those bags Tuffy carried mail and tools and sometimes medicines to the aquanauts below. Up, down, up, down, he swam — the only live link between two very different worlds.

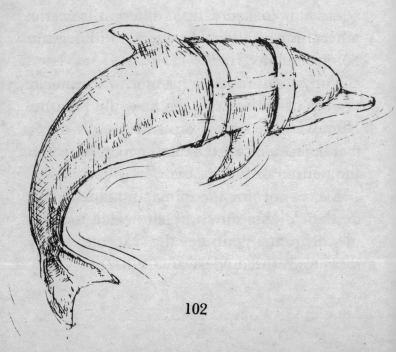

Tuffy had been trained to do another job too. It was the most important of all. He had been trained to save lives.

The human aquanauts were safe inside Sealab. They had all sorts of comforts there — hot food, water, soft beds, books, even television. But the minute they stepped outside they entered a strange and dangerous world.

The sun often shone brightly on the top of the water. But it was always dark as night 60 metres below, where the human aquanauts were exploring.

Each aquanaut carried two small tanks of air on his back. That air meant the difference between life and death in this world of water. But what if an aquanaut got lost? What if he couldn't find his way back to the safety of Sealab before his air was used up?

The human aquanauts knew that if this happened they had one last hope. Tuffy. None of the men became lost during the Sealab II project. But they weren't taking any chances. Again and again they ran tests. They pretended to be lost.

A man would hide himself behind a rock or in the middle of a big clump of plants. He would set off a special buzzer he always carried with him. This buzzer could be heard on the surface of the water. "Emergency!" it meant. "A man is lost. We need Tuffy! Fast!"

Seconds later Tuffy would come plunging down through the water. But he wouldn't

head for the "lost" aquanaut — not right away. First he would swim to the Sealab capsule. He would slide his snout through a ring. The ring was attached to one end of a long rope. The other end of the rope was hooked to the metal side of Sealab.

Now *creee-eeeKKKKK*. Tuffy would scan the water with his sonar. Then off he'd swim towards the hiding man, trailing the rope

behind him. Seconds later the man would take the ring from Tuffy. Now he could follow the lifeline of rope back to Sealab — and safety. And Tuffy? His job was done. So he would head for the top of the water for a welcome gulp of air.

Usually Tuffy made this round-trip of rescue in about one minute. Did he always do his job so quickly and so well? Yes . . . except once.

Tuffy was a very clever, very hard-working dolphin. But he was also stubborn. And he loved to eat. So when Tuffy brought the ring to an aquanaut he was always given a reward. Each man carried a small plastic bag of chopped fish. Tuffy would let the man take the ring. Then the man would squirt some fish into Tuffy's mouth.

But once something went wrong. The aquanaut tugged and tugged, but he couldn't get his bag of fish open. So finally he gave Tuffy a shove. "Move on," he meant.

But Tuffy didn't move on. *Where was his reward? Where was his mouthful of fish? This wasn't the way things were supposed to happen!*

Tuffy stared at the man for a moment. He raised one of his flippers and bopped him over the head. *Then* the dolphin aquanaut swam on.

JUGGLERS

There are books to suit everyone in Hippo's JUGGLERS series:

When I Lived Down Cuckoo Lane
by Jean Wills   £1.75
A small girl and her family move into a new house in Cuckoo Lane. Follow her adventures through the year as she makes friends, starts a new school, learns to ride a bike, and even helps out at her father's shop.

The Secret of Bone Island by Sam McBratney   £1.75
Linda, Peter and Gareth are very curious about Bone Island. Especially when they're told some weird stories about the island's history. And then three suspicious-looking men warn them to stay away from the island . . .

Stan's Galactic Bug by John Emlyn Edwards   £1.75
Stan can't believe his eyes when his computer game traps an alien from outer space. It's up to Stan to save the intergalactic traveller from destruction!

As If By Magic by Jo Furminger   £1.75
Natasha has never seen a girl as weird as Harriet – the new girl in the class. But not only does she *look* strange, with her dark tatty clothes and bright green eyes, but the oddest things start to happen when she's around.

Bags of trouble by Michael Harrison   £1.75
Matthew's weekend starts off badly when he's roped into helping at the school jumble sale. Then he finds out that the Mozart cassette he buys at the sale is actually a computer tape. And when he runs the tape, what he discovers threatens to turn his weekend into a disaster!

The Jiggery-Pokery Cup by Angela Bull   £1.75
Kelly is determined to win the Lady Jiggins-Povey Cup.
She always tries hard at the village show competitions, but
she never wins any prizes. Her brothers know she doesn't
have a hope of winning without some help, and so decide to
try a little "jiggery-pokery" to help her along . . .

Look out for these other titles in the JUGGLERS series:

The Ghosts of Batwing Castle by Terry Deary
The Pet Minders by Robina Beckles Willson

STREAMERS

We've got lots of great books for younger readers in Hippo's STREAMERS series:

Sally Ann – On Her Own by Terrance Dicks £1.75
Sally Ann is a very special toy. She's a rag doll who likes to be involved in everything that's going on. When Sally Ann finds out that the nursery school where she lives might be closed down, she decides it's time to take action!

Sally Ann – The School Play by Terrance Dicks£1.75
When the nursery school's electricity goes off, Sally Ann comes up with a wonderful idea to pay for the new wiring. But not everything runs as smoothly as Sally Ann would like!

The Little Yellow Taxi and His Friends
by Ruth Ainsworth £1.75
The little grey car can't get to sleep at night, and keeps all the other cars and lorries awake. So the garage owner paints the little car yellow, gives him a sign for his roof, and turns him into an all-night taxi.

Tom by Ruth Silvestre £1.75
The circus has come to town, and Tom tries to tell his parents about it. But they are always too busy to listen. . . A delightful collection of stories about Tom, his family and friends.

Nate the Great by Marjorie Weinman Sharmat £1.75
Nate the Great is a detective. Who likes pancakes. And solving mysteries. When his friend Annie asks him to help her find a missing picture, Nate the Great sets about solving the most challenging case of his career.

Nate the Great and the Missing Key
by Marjorie Weinman Sharmat £1.75
Nate the Great, master sleuth and pancake authority, is on the trail of another puzzling mystery. Annie wants to give a birthday party for her dog, Fang, but she can't find the key. It's up to Nate to solve the riddle of Rosamond's strange poem and track down the missing key.